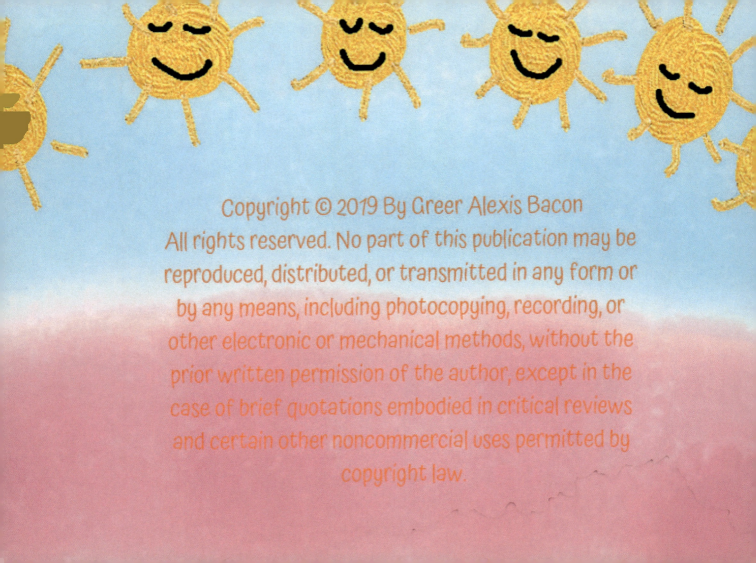

Copyright © 2019 By Greer Alexis Bacon

All rights reserved. No part of this publication may be reproduced, distributed, or transmitted in any form or by any means, including photocopying, recording, or other electronic or mechanical methods, without the prior written permission of the author, except in the case of brief quotations embodied in critical reviews and certain other noncommercial uses permitted by copyright law.

And God said, "Let there be lights in the expanse of the heavens to separate the day from the night. And let them be for signs and for seasons, and for days and years,
Genesis 1:14

The flowers and trees count on you because you help them stay tall and green.

you might be closer to the stars in the night time sky.

Just so you know, planet Earth counts on you too!

from the deer in the forest

to the frogs on the lillypad,

Each animal loves the warmth you give them.

I know you are there when the skies are snowy,

I know you are there when the skies are rainy.

you are twice as pretty when there is a rainbow.

you give us sunrises;

you leave as sunsets.

All fruits need your light;

All veggies need your warmth.

Thank you, sun, for being so bright and bringing us warmth and light!

About the Author

Greer Alexis Bacon, a native of Westchester NY. lives today in the Finger Lake region of New York State. Where she and her husband raise their two children. Since 2005, Greer has been writing as a hobby. Ten years later, she continues to write children's books. Greer's First Published book: Guardian, where a dream is challenged, was first written in 2005. And wasn't until the winter of 2015, when Greer competed her book with illustrations. She plans to continue her love for writing for years to come. she will love to hear from her fans like you! email her at: greerbacon@gmail.com

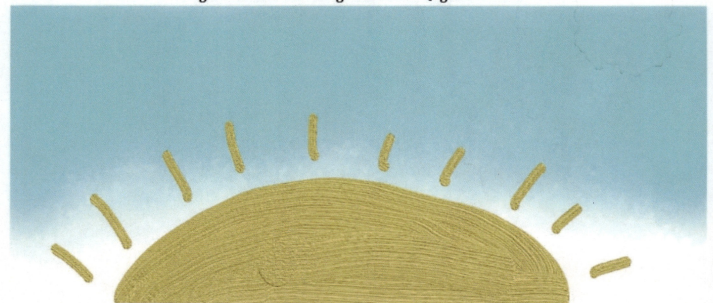

Made in the USA
Middletown, DE
29 May 2019